W9-ATM-439

SOME IMPORTANT PLACES IN FRIDA KAHLO'S LIFE

1. **Mexico**. Even though Frida Kahlo occasionally traveled to other countries, she spent most of her life living and working in Mexico. Frida was greatly influenced by the art, crafts, music, food, people, and history of her country. She loved joining in Mexico's many national celebrations and festivals, and was active in Mexico's politics.

2. **Mexico City**. Frida was born and lived in the town of Coyoacán, now a district of Mexico City, the capital city of Mexico. Today Coyoacán is an important historical center of Mexico City, known for its many museums, plazas, and beautiful buildings and churches. Some of them were built almost 500 years ago!

THIS IS THE AREA THAT'S SHOWN ON THE LARGER MAP

MAP OF THE ENTIRE TOTAL COMPLETE WORLD

TIMELINE OF FRIDA KAHLO'S LIFE

1907 Frida Kahlo is born on July 6 in Coyoacán, Mexico.

1913 At age six, Frida contracts polio, a paralyzing disease. She works hard for the next few years to get her strength back.

1922 Frida enters the National Preparatory School, one of the best high schools in Mexico. Two years later Frida spots famous artist Diego Rivera as he is painting a mural at the school. Frida has no idea that years later she will end up marrying Diego.

1925 Frida is involved in a terrible bus accident. She recovers, but her injuries cause her serious health problems for the rest of her life.

1926 While recovering from the accident, Frida is confined to her bed. She teaches herself to paint as a way to help pass the time.

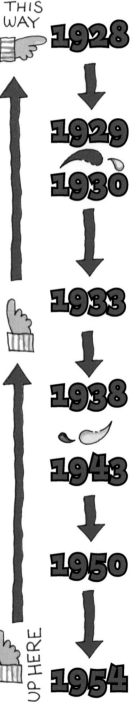

THIS WAY

UP HERE

1928 Frida is officially introduced to Diego Rivera at a party. Diego likes Frida's paintings and encourages her to do more.

1929 Frida marries Diego Rivera. She becomes a full-time artist.

1930 Over the next three years, Frida travels to San Francisco, Detroit, and New York City to be with Diego while he paints murals in each city.

1933 Frida returns to Mexico and gets back to work. Her paintings become more and more popular.

1938 Frida is invited to show her work in New York City, Paris, France, and Mexico.

1943 A busy Frida continues getting attention for her artwork, and begins teaching students at a new art school.

1950 Frida's health worsens. She spends most of this year in the hospital. When home, she often paints and teaches her students from her bed.

1954 Frida Kahlo dies in Coyoacán on July 13.

GETTING TO KNOW THE WORLD'S GREATEST ARTISTS

F R I D A
KAHLO

WRITTEN AND ILLUSTRATED BY MIKE VENEZIA

CHILDREN'S PRESS®

An Imprint of Scholastic Inc.

For Mike and Liz

Cover: *The Frame or Self Portrait*, Ca. 1938. Oil on aluminum,
under glass and painted wood, 28.5 x 20.5 cm. Photograph ©
Jean-Claude Planchet/CNAC/MNAM/Dist. RMN-Grand Palais/Art
Resource, NY.

© 2015 Banco de México Diego Rivera & Frida Kahlo Museums
Trust, Mexico, D.F./Artists Rights Society (ARS), New York

Library of Congress Cataloging-in-Publication Data

Venezia, Mike.
 Frida Kahlo / by Mike Venezia. — Revised Edition.
   pages cm. — (Getting to know the world's greatest artists)
Includes bibliographical references and index.
 ISBN 978-0-531-21259-2 (library binding) —
ISBN 978-0-531-21321-6 (pbk.)
 1. Kahlo, Frida–Juvenile literature. 2. Painters–Mexico–
Biography—Juvenile literature. I. Title.
 ND259.K33V46 2015
 759.972—dc23
 [B]   2015020971

No part of this publication may be reproduced in whole or in part, or stored in a retrieval
system, or transmitted in any form or by any means, electronic, mechanical, photocopying,
recording, or otherwise, without written permission of the publisher. For information
regarding permission, write to Scholastic Inc., 557 Broadway, New York, NY 10012.

©2016 by Mike Venezia Inc.

All rights reserved. Published in 2016 by Children's Press, an imprint of Scholastic Inc.
Printed in China 62

SCHOLASTIC, CHILDREN'S PRESS, and associated logos are trademarks and/or
registered trademarks of Scholastic Inc.

4 5 6 7 8 9 10 R 25 24 23 22 21 20 19 18

Scholastic Inc., 557 Broadway, New York, NY 10012.

Photograph of Frida Kahlo. Photo by Nickolas Muray; © Nickolas Muray Photo Archives.

Frida Kahlo was one of the greatest artists of the twentieth century. She was born in Coyoacán, Mexico, in 1907. Frida grew up during the Mexican Revolution, an event that influenced her life and changed the art of Mexico forever.

Self-Portrait Dedicated to Leon Trotsky, 1937. Frida Kahlo. Oil on Masonite, 30 x 24 in. Photograph by Lee Stalsworth / Courtesy of the National Museum of Women in the Arts, Washington, D.C. / Gift of the Honorable Clare Boothe Luce.

Some of Frida's most famous works are self-portraits. In many of them she shows herself surrounded by things that were important to her.

Self-Portrait with Changuito, by Frida Kahlo. 1945.
Fundación Dolores Olmedo, Mexico City, Mexico.
Photograph © Schalkwijk/Art Resource, NY.

Self-Portrait with Loose Hair, by Frida Kahlo. 1947.
© Christie's Images/Superstock, Inc.

Frida especially liked
to paint flowers, plants,
forests, animals,
costumes, jewelry, and
ancient gods and
idols that were found
only in Mexico.

Frida often showed unpleasant things that happened during her life. These paintings are sometimes shocking to people. But Frida needed to paint them to help her get through some hard times.

The painting shown on the next page, *Without Hope,* was done after a serious illness. Frida had grown weak and had no appetite. Her doctors wanted her to eat lots of strained foods. Frida was disgusted by the idea of being forced to eat, and showed how she felt about this in her painting. Frida painted most of these disturbing pictures for herself. She was surprised when anyone else showed any interest in them.

Sin Esperanza (Without Hope), by Frida Kahlo. 1945. Photograph © Schalkwijk/Art Resource, NY.

Frida Kahlo went through a lot of pain and suffering during her life. When she was six years old, she caught a serious disease called polio. She got better, but the disesase left her right leg thin and weak.

To help improve her leg, Frida's parents got her to do lots of physical activities, including soccer, swimming , bicycling, and even boxing!

Frida (at left, standing) with some members of her family. 1926. Guillermo Kahlo. © Reproduction authorized by Instituto Nacional de Bellas Artes y Literatura / Centro Nacional de las Artes, Biblioteca de las Artes, Mexico.

Nothing seemed to help, though. Kids in the neighborhood started calling her "Frida peg leg."

Frida wore long dresses and pants to hide her leg. She never wanted anyone to know she was different, or feel sorry for her, or make fun of her.

Frida Kahlo was very curious as a child. She especially wanted to know about nature and science. Her father thought this was great, and encouraged Frida to learn as much as she could.

El Castillo Chichén Itzá (Mayan), Yucatan, Mexico.
Photograph © Superstock, Inc.

Retrato de mi Padre, Wilhelm Kahlo,
by Frida Kahlo. 1952. Oil on masonite.
60 x 46 cm. Colección Museo Frida
Kahlo. © Reproduction authorized
by Instituto Nacional de Bellas Artes
y Literatura/Centro Nacional de las
Artes, Biblioteca de las Artes, Mexico.

Frida was always bringing home plants, rocks, insects, and small animals to study. Mr. Kahlo was a professional photographer and an amateur artist who was also curious about all kinds of things. He taught his daughter about ancient Mexican art and architecture. Mr. Kahlo showed Frida how to use a camera and how to retouch and color photographs. These things came in handy later, when Frida became an artist.

11

Frida attended one of the best high
schools in the country. It was located right
in the middle of Mexico City. In high school,
Frida learned how important the Mexican
Revolution was to the people of her country.

Zapata's Agrarian Revolution, by David Alfaro Siqueiros. Fresco. Museo Nacional de Historia,
Mexico City. Photograph © Giraudon/Art Resource, NY.

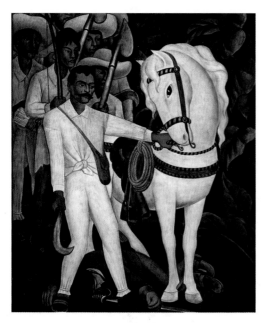

Agrarian Leader Zapata, by Diego Rivera. 1931. Fresco. 238.1 x 188 cm. Abby Aldrich Rockefeller Fund. © Museum of Modern Art, New York.

Before the Revolution, thousands of people were treated like slaves. They were very poor and uneducated, and most worked on farms all day long. A few greedy government officials and farm owners kept all the money for themselves.

In 1910, the Mexican people, with leaders like Pancho Villa and Emiliano Zapata, rebelled against the Mexican government and won the right to make life fair for everyone in Mexico.

Triumph of the Revolution-Distribution of Food (Triunfo de la Revolución, reparto de los alimentos), by Diego Rivera. 1926-27. Fresco. 3.54 x 3.67 m. Chapel, Universidad Autónoma Chapingo, Chapingo, Mexico. Photograph © Schalkwijk/Art Resource, NY.

13

The Trench, by José Clemente Orozco. Escuela Nacional Preparatoria San Ildefonso, Mexico City, Mexico. Photograph © Schalkwijk/Art Resource, NY.

Huelga de Cananea, by David Alfaro Siqueiros. Museo Nacional de Historia, Castillo de Chapultepec, Mexico City, Mexico. Photograph © Schalkwijk/Art Resource, NY.

One of the first things the new Mexican government did was hire artists to paint large scenes on the walls of public buildings for everyone to see. These paintings, called murals, showed the history of Mexico. They were meant to help uneducated people understand their past, make them proud of their country, and give them hope for the future.

The Totonac Civilization, by Diego Rivera. 1942. Mural. 4.92 x 5.27 m. Patio Corridor, National Palace, Mexico City, Mexico. Photograph © Schalkwijk/Art Resource, NY.

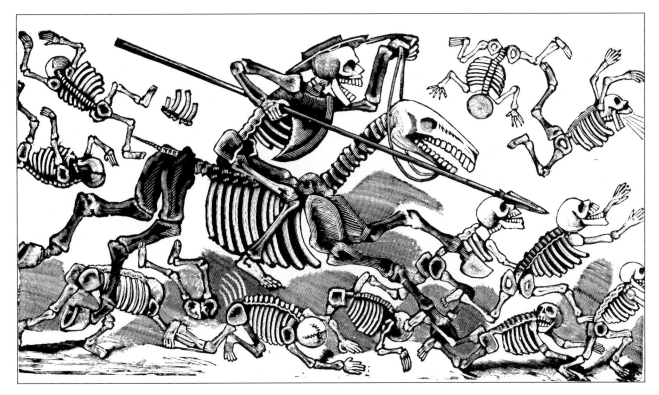

Calavera de Don Quijote, by José Guadalupe Posada. Engraving. © Posada's Popular Mexican Prints, 1972, Dover Publications.

The most famous mural artists were David Siqueiros, José Orozco, and Diego Rivera. These painters were inspired by the art and colors of ancient Mexican civilizations. They were also influenced by Mexican popular art, like the lively prints of José Posada. They purposely kept away from European-influenced art, which was the accepted style of art before the Mexican Revolution.

Creation, by Diego Rivera. Fresco. Escuela Nacional Preparatoria, Anfiteatro Bolívar, Mexico City, Mexico. Photograph © Detroit Institute of Arts.

When Frida was fourteen years old, Diego Rivera came to her school to paint one of his murals. In high school, Frida was known as a troublemaker. She made herself a pain in the

neck to her teachers and anyone else in authority, including the famous Diego. Frida played tricks on Diego and called out names, like "old fatso," while he was trying to work.

El accidente 17 de septiembre de 1926, by Frida Kahlo. 1926. Pencil on paper. 20 x 27 cm. Colección Rafael Coronel. © Reproduction authorized by Instituto Nacional de Bellas Artes y Literatura/Centro Nacional de las Artes, Biblioteca de las Artes, Mexico.

Frida wasn't all that interested in art until a very bad thing happened to her. One day, on the way home from school, the bus she was riding got into a terrible accident. Some people were even killed. Frida was badly injured and had to spend months in bed. Her bones never really healed properly. She had lots of pain and had to have many operations during her life.

It was at this time that Frida decided to take up art. She was bored lying in bed and needed something to do. Frida borrowed her father's paints and brushes. Her mother had a special easel made so Frida could work while she was lying on her back. Frida started by painting portraits of her friends, family, and the subject she knew best: herself.

Autorretrato, by Frida Kahlo. 1926. Oil on masonite. 78 x 61 cm. Colección Instituto Tlaxcalteca de Cultura, Tlaxcala, Mexico. © Reproduction authorized by Instituto Nacional de Bellas Artes y Literatura/Centro Nacional de las Artes, Biblioteca de las Artes, Mexico.

Cafe Singer, by Amedeo Modigliani. Canvas.
92.4 x 60.3 cm. Chester Dale Collection.
© National Gallery of Art, Washington, DC.

At first, Frida was her own teacher. She studied her father's art books and copied the paintings of great European artists like Sandro Botticelli and Amedeo Modigliani. But soon, just like the Mexican mural artists, Frida became more interested in the folk art of her own country. Frida loved the energy of these works of art and the simple stories they told.

Santo Niño de Atocha, by unknown artist. Oil on tin.
12 3/4 x 9 3/4 in. © Rights & Reproduction
Department San Antonio Museum of Art.

San Francisco de Paula
Ex-Voto, by unknown
artist. Oil on tin Retablo.
7 x 10 in. The Nelson
A. Rockefeller Mexican
Folk Art Collection.
© Rights & Reproduction
Department San Antonio
Museum of Art.

Comenso á estar enferma de mucha gravedad Maria Blaza Vasquez de
una fuerte decenteria y durante cuatro meses y no haijando rremedio en lo tem
poral la madre de dicha niña Ocurrio al auxilio de S. S. Francisco de Paula
de la Compaña quien le á rrestablecido la Salud, Guanajuato Mzo. de 1859.

These paintings and prints seemed filled with
the magic that many people in Mexico felt was
a real part of their everyday lives. She found
a mysterious power in religious paintings and
ancient Mexican Indian art. Frida began to
include in her own paintings the things that she
discovered
in Mexican
folk art.

The Bus (El Camion), by Frida
Kahlo. 1929. Oil on canvas.
26 x 55 cm. Fundación
Dolores Olmedo, Mexico
City, D. F., Mexico.
Photograph © Schalkwijk/
Art Resource, NY.

Birth of Class Consciousness (El Agitador), by Diego Rivera. 1926-27. Mural. 2.44 x 5.53 m. Chapel, Universidad Autónoma Chapingo, Chapingo, Mexico. Photograph © Schalkwijk/Art Resource, NY.

Frida enjoyed painting. It made her feel better. Soon she felt well enough to get around again. Frida made up her mind then never to let her pain and injuries get in the way of having fun. She kept working on her paintings, got together with friends, and went to lots of parties.

At one party, she was introduced to Diego Rivera. He didn't remember Frida because she was grown up now and looked much different.

Diego did remember her, though, a few days later, when she came to see him while he was painting one of his murals. Frida wanted to show Diego some of her artwork to see what he thought. Even though Frida had teased him years before, she had always been fascinated by Diego and respected his talent.

Portrait of Galicia Galant, by Frida Kahlo. 1927.
Fundación Dolores Olmedo, Mexico City, D. F.,
Mexico. Photograph. © Schalkwijk/Art Resource, NY.

Frida and Diego on their wedding day, August, 21,
1929. © Víctor Reyes y Familia /Reproduction
authorized by Instituto Nacional de Bellas Artes y
Literatura/Centro Nacional de las Artes, Biblioteca
de las Artes, Mexico.

Diego thought Frida's
artwork was great.
Now that Frida was
grown up, he thought she was great, too.
Frida invited Diego to her home to look
at other paintings she had done.

Diego visited the Kahlo home often.
He and Frida got to know each other well
and started dating. After a while, they fell
in love. Even though Diego was more than
twenty years older than Frida, they decided
to get married.

Frida Kahlo and Diego Rivera. 1931. Photograph © Peter Juley. Colección Museo Frida Kahlo © Reproduction authorized by Instituto Nacional de Bellas Artes y Literatura/Centro Nacional de las Artes, Biblioteca de las Artes, Mexico.

Diego always encouraged Frida with her art. He was proud of his talented wife. Frida learned a lot from Diego. He turned out to be an excellent art teacher.

Now Frida Kahlo was the wife of one of the most famous artists in the world. At first it was fine with her to just take care of her husband. Frida enjoyed being with Diego every day while he worked. But she wasn't doing much of her own artwork.

In the 1930s, Diego was asked to paint murals in the United States. Diego and Frida traveled there often and were admired wherever they went. They looked great together and were fun to be around. Frida and Diego were always being invited to the parties of rich and famous people.

Diego Rivera and Frida Kahlo in Coyoacán. 1931. Fotografía y Colección de Mrs. Frances Flynn Paine © Reproduction authorized by Instituto Nacional de Bellas Artes y Literatura/Centro Nacional de las Artes, Biblioteca de las Artes, Mexico.

Frida and Diego Rivera, by Frida Kahlo. 1931. Oil on canvas. 100 x 78.7 cm. Albert M. Bender Collection. Gift of Albert M. Bender. © San Francisco Museum of Modern Art.

Things didn't always go well between Diego and Frida, though. They often had serious arguments. One disagreement was over how much time they were spending in the United States. Diego loved the modern American cities, but Frida didn't enjoy being there at all. She was homesick and wanted to get back to Mexico.

Frida did the painting on the next page to show her feelings about the United States. She painted an overcrowded New York City filled with factories, garbage, and pollution. There's no sign of Frida in this picture. She has probably returned to Mexico, leaving only her dress behind.

My Dress Hangs Here, by Frida Kahlo. 1933-38. © Christie's Images/Superstock, Inc.

Sometimes, after a serious argument, Frida and Diego would live apart from each other. During these times, Frida painted more often, and created some of her best works.

Self-Portrait with Cropped Hair, by Frida Kahlo. 1940. Oil on canvas. 40 x 27.9 cm. Gift of Edgar Kaufmann, Jr. © Museum of Modern Art, New York.

The Two Fridas, by Frida Kahlo. 1939. Museo Nacional de Arte Moderno, Mexico City, Mexico. Photograph © Schalkwijk/Art Resource, NY.

Frida Kahlo painted her real feelings in a way that had never been seen before. As time went on, her work started to become as well known as her famous husband's. Frida was able to show her happiness, disappointment, and pain. Her paintings are filled with Mexican colors and images that could have come only from someone who loved their country as much as she did.

The Frame or Self Portrait, Ca. 1938. Oil on aluminum, under glass and painted wood, 28.5 x 20.5 cm. Photograph © Jean-Claude Planchet/CNAC/MNAM/Dist. RMN-Grand Palais/Art Resource, NY.

Frida Kahlo's health was a serious problem throughout her life. She died in 1954. But early on, Frida had decided to enjoy life as much as possible. She always spent a lot of time fixing her hair and dressing in beautiful costumes. Some of her friends said that when she was finished, she had become almost a piece of art herself.

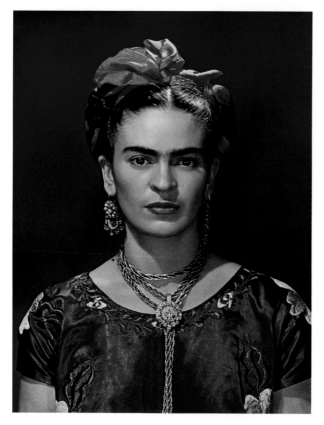

Photograph of Frida Kahlo. Photo by Nickolas Muray; © Nickolas Muray Photo Archive.

Works of art in this book can be seen at the following places:

Escuela Nacional Preparatoria San Ildefonso, Mexico City, Mexico
Instituto Tlaxcalteca de Cultura, Tlaxcala, Mexico
Musée National d'Art Moderne, Paris, France
Museo Frida Kahlo, Mexico City, Mexico
Museo Nacional de Arte Moderno, Mexico City, Mexico
Museo Nacional de Historia, Mexico City, Mexico
The Museum of Modern Art, New York, New York
National Gallery of Art, Washington, D.C.
National Museum of Women in the Arts, Washington, D.C.
National Palace, Mexico City, Mexico
San Antonio Museum of Art, San Antonio, Texas
San Francisco Museum of Modern Art, San Francisco, California
Universidad Autonoma Chapingo, Chapingo, Mexico

LEARN MORE BY TAKING THE KAHLO QUIZ!

(ANSWERS ON THE NEXT PAGE.)

1. Frida Kahlo was a member of which of the following important art groups?
  ⓐ The Impressionists
  ⓑ The Surrealists
  ⓒ The Cubists
  ⓓ The Mexican Home Design Group
  ⓔ None of the above

2. What were some of Frida's favorite pets she kept around the house?
  ⓐ Amazon parrots
  ⓑ A small deer
  ⓒ An eagle
  ⓓ Hairless Mexican Xoloitzcuintli dogs
  ⓔ Spider monkeys
  ⓕ All of the above

3. Even though Frida Kahlo had health problems, she always tried to keep her spirits up. Aside from painting, what were some of her favorite feel-good activities?
  ⓐ Synchronized ice-skating
  ⓑ Throwing parties
  ⓒ Cooking
  ⓓ Playing golf

4. Why did Frida and Diego paint their house bright blue?
  ⓐ To cover up stains left from a blueberry pie-eating contest that got out of hand.
  ⓑ To help Frida's pet bluebirds camouflage themselves from natural predators.
  ⓒ To ward off evil spirits.
  ⓓ They just liked blue.

5. If you look closely at the painting on page 30 of this book, *The Two Fridas*, you can see Frida knew a lot about medical illustrating. Where did Frida learn this skill?
  ⓐ In grade school, Frida's father bought her an X-ray machine so she could study the workings of the human body.
  ⓑ At one time, Frida studied to be a doctor and showed a talent for making medical illustrations.
  ⓒ Frida loved watching gory horror movies.

ANSWERS

1. **e** An independent Frida Kahlo refused to be linked to any art movement or group. Her paintings were very personal and original.

2. **f** Frida was crazy about animals! She also had pet cats, parakeets, macaws, hens, and sparrows. You can see many of Frida's pets in her self-portraits.

3. **b and c** Frida loved to celebrate holidays, birthdays, and special events of all kinds. Almost every month she cooked wonderful Mexican dishes and arranged parties with music and fun decorations. Her house was open to friends, family members, and even neighbors who happened to be passing by.

4. **c** According to Mexican folk legend, bright blue was thought to ward off evil spirits. Today, Frida's Blue House is open to the public as the Frida Kahlo Museum.

5. **b** In high school, Frida thought she might want to be a doctor. She studied medicine and medical illustration. Frida learned a lot about drawing the human body at that time.

HEY, WHAT DOES THAT WORD MEAN?

ancient (AYN-shunt) Very old

architecture (AR-ki-tek-chur) The style in which buildings are designed

disturbing (diss-TURB-ing) Upsetting

encourage (en-KUR-ij) To give someone confidence by supporting that person

idol (EYE-duhl) An image or statue worshipped as a god

mural (MYU-ruhl) A painting done directly on a wall

print (PRINT) A printed copy of a painting or drawing

polio (POH-lee-oh) An infectious disease that can cause paralysis

rebel (ri-BEL) To struggle against the people in charge

retouch (ree-TUHCH) To improve by making slight changes

revolution (rev-uh-LOO-shuhn) An uprising by the people of a country that changes its system of government

self-portrait (SELF-POR-trit) A drawing, painting, or photograph of oneself

Visit this Scholastic Web site for more information on Kahlo:
www.factsfornow.scholastic.com
Enter the keyword Kahlo

INDEX